VICTORIA & ALBER

Chinese Porcelain
of the Ch'ing Dynasty

LONDON

HER MAJESTY'S STATIONERY OFFICE

1957

INTRODUCTION

THE wares here illustrated were made during the reigns of three great Emperors of the Ch'ing dynasty – K'ang Hsi (1662–1722), his son Yung Chêng (1723–35), and his grandson Ch'ien Lung (1736–95).

From the beginning of the Ming dynasty (1368–1644) the potteries of Ching-tê Chên in Kiangsi Province became the most important in China. The beautiful white porcelain made here from local deposits of china clay (kaolin) and china stone (petuntse) was supplied by Imperial kilns to the court, and by numerous other factories to markets in China, the Near East, and eventually Europe. In the troubled decades before and after the fall of the Ming in 1644 the Imperial kilns closed down, and the great revival began with their rebuilding in 1683.

Many of the techniques now developed had been used before, and imitations of Ming vessels or Emperors' marks bear witness to the respect in which these were still held. Compared with the best Ming wares the Ch'ing porcelains may lack profundity in design and thoroughness in drawing; as in contemporary European baroque and eighteenth-century art, the emphasis is on general decorative effect. According to the Jesuit missionary Père d'Entrecolles, who recorded his observations at Ching-tê Chên in two long letters dated 1712 and 1722, labour at the factories was so subdivided that a vase might pass through seventy different hands, inevitably losing the strong impress of any particular artist. Nevertheless, the Ch'ing porcelains will always rank among the greatest achievements of the potter, whether for their inherent beauties of design, or for the amazing accomplishment of their execution in a very wide range of techniques. They were a constant inspiration to European potters in the seventeenth and eighteenth centuries, and it is only within the last generation that their merits have risked being overlooked, owing to the fashionable enthusiasm for Chinese wares of earlier periods. The Victoria & Albert Museum possesses one of the finest existing collections, enriched as it is by the incomparable Salting Bequest.

In the reign of K'ang Hsi particular attention was paid to the large vases, whose monumental grandeur of form, with its emphasis on height, was matched by a vigorous abandon in the painted decoration. A contrasting ideal of smooth perfection and calculated refinement was especially pursued in the reign of Yung Chêng, with some loss of force; many pieces were made of a very thin 'eggshell' porcelain. Under Ch'ien Lung a decline of taste gradually became evident in the often perverse ingenuity of forms and unusual colour-effects.

Most famous among the many monochrome glazes were the 'peach-bloom', *sang de bœuf*, and *rouge flambé* derived from copper (1). (The names now used for these and other colour-effects were first given by French collectors in the second half of the nineteenth century.) The beautiful creamy-white porcelain made at Tê-hua in Fukien province stands apart from the Ching-tê Chên wares: it was used with the happiest effect for figures (2, 3).

Some rare pieces dating from the early years of K'ang Hsi's reign have delicately pencilled figure-subjects in underglaze violet-blue like those found on a class made since the late Ming period for export as well as for non-Imperial use in China (6). But in the typical K'ang Hsi 'blue-and-white' made after 1683 the cobalt colour, applied in graded washes, is of a cool intensity unmatched before or since (4–9). It appears at its best in the vases painted with prunus-blossom against a dark background of crackled ice (5).

Much of the painting was done in easily fusible 'enamel' colours, applied after the vessel had received its preliminary firing. Under K'ang Hsi the favourite colour-scheme was the *famille verte*, with its transparent greens and fiery iron-reds (12–23); in the rare *famille jaune* and *famille noire* vases the background of the design was filled in with yellow, or with black under a coat of transparent green (10, 11). A peculiarly soft and harmonious effect was often obtained by painting the enamels directly on to the body of the vessel without an intervening glaze ('enamel on the biscuit'). The *famille rose* colour scheme favoured from the time of Yung Chêng onwards is characterized by the use of rose-crimson derived from gold, and by opaque white, yellow and greyish green (24, 26). (The crimson, and possibly other colours, were introduced from Europe.) Much Yung Chêng and Ch'ien Lung enamelled porcelain is painted in a detailed and somewhat stereotyped miniature style which may be contrasted with the usually freer manner practised under K'ang Hsi (26–28).

A. L.

1. Vase, brownish-red glaze mottled with 'peach-bloom'. Mark and reign of K'ang Hsi. Ht. 11 in. Salting Bequest.   c. 362–1910

2. Figure of the Goddess Kuan Yin; Fukien white porcelain.
Mark, *I Mo-tzŭ*, impressed. 17th or 18th century. Ht. 15⅛ in.
Salting Bequest.   c. 548–1910

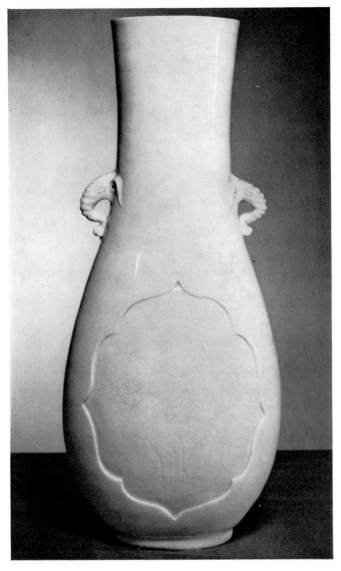

3. Vase, Fukien white porcelain. 17th or 18th century. Ht. 16⅜ in.
Henry L. Florence Bequest.   c. 1296–1917

4. Vase, with magnolias carved in low-relief and painted in underglaze blue. Reign of K'ang Hsi. Ht. 17⅞ in. Salting Bequest.　　　　c. 829–1910

5. Bottle, painted with prunus-blossom, in underglaze blue.
Reign of K'ang Hsi. Ht. 17 in. Salting Bequest. c. 791–1910

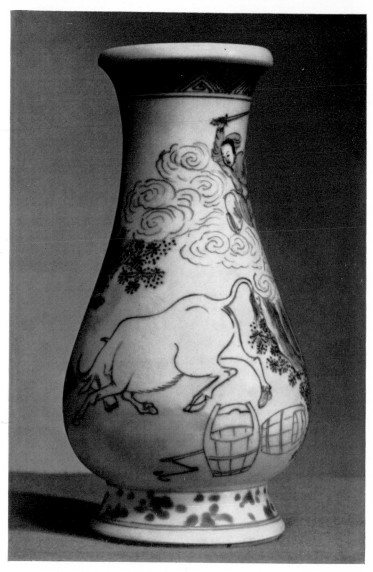

6. Vase, painted in underglaze blue. A god striking two cows with madness. Mark of Ch'êng Hua; reign of K'ang Hsi. Ht. $5\frac{7}{8}$ in. Salting Bequest.   c. 876–1910

7. Jar, painted with a mythical beast, in underglaze blue. Reign of
K'ang Hsi. Ht. 7⅞ in. Salting Bequest.   c. 920–1910

8. Plate, painted with a hunting-scene, in underglaze blue. Mark of Ch'êng Hua; reign of K'ang Hsi. D. 7¾ in. Salting Bequest.

c. 694–1910

9. Plate, painted with a picnic, in underglaze blue. Mark of Ch'êng Hua; reign of K'ang Hsi. D. 6⅜ in. Salting Bequest.   c. 709-1910

10. Vase, painted with birds and plum-blossom, black ground (*famille noire*). Reign of K'ang Hsi. Ht. 24½ in. Salting Bequest.

c. 1307–1910

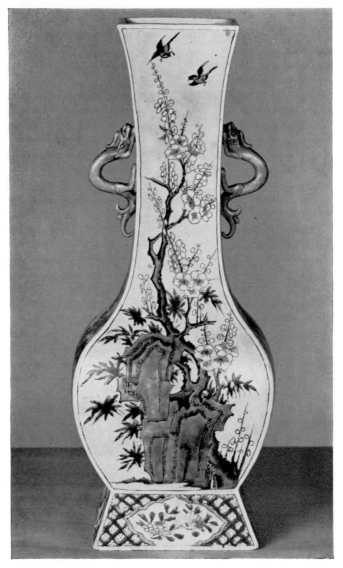

11. Vase, painted 'on the biscuit' with flowering trees, yellow ground (*famille jaune*). Reign of K'ang Hsi. Ht. 20½ in. Salting Bequest.

c. 1284–1910

12. Vase, painted in colours of the *famille verte*. Reign of K'ang Hsi. Ht. 23¾ in. Salting Bequest.   c. 1298–1910

13. Vase, painted in colours of the *famille verte*, with a garden scene. Reign of K'ang Hsi. Ht. 18 in. Salting Bequest.

c. 1251–1910

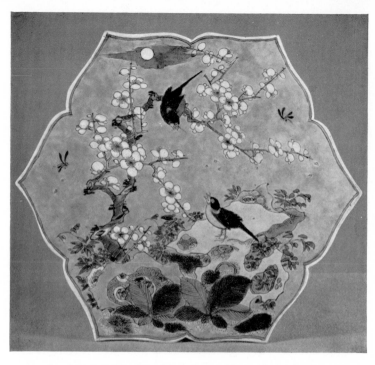

14. Stand, painted 'on the biscuit' in colours of the *famille verte*.
Reign of K'ang Hsi. D. 9⅞ in. Salting Bequest.   c. 1083–1910

15. Stand, painted 'on the biscuit' in colours of the *famille verte*.
Reign of K'ang Hsi. D. 10 in. Salting Bequest.   c. 1050–1910

16. Figure of the war-god, Kuan-Ti. Painted 'on the biscuit' in colours of the *famille verte*. Reign of K'ang Hsi. Ht. 11¼ in. Salting Bequest.　　　c. 1071–1910

(*Left*) Water-pot in form of a rat and vine. Ht. 3⅜ in.

c. 1093–1910

(*Below*) Tea-pot. Ht. 4¼ in.

c. 1095–1910

17. Painted 'on the biscuit' in colours of the *famille verte*. Reign of K'ang Hsi. Salting Bequest.

18. Painted in colours of the *famille verte*. Reign of K'ang Hsi. Salting Bequest.

(*Above*) Bowl with agricultural scenes. D. 7¼ in.　　c. 1269–1910

(*Below*) Bowl with hunting-scene. Mark of K'ang Hsi. D. 8¼ in.

　　　　　　　　　　　　　　　　　　　　　　c. 1267–1910

19. Plate, painted in colours of the *famille verte*, and inscribed with birthday wishes. Mark and reign of K'ang Hsi. Perhaps made for the Emperor's sixtieth birthday in 1713. D. 10 in.   c. 3–1947

20. Dish, painted with a battle-scene in colours of the *famille verte*.
Mark, an artemisia-leaf. Reign of K'ang Hsi. D. 14⅝ in. Salting
Bequest.   c. 1221–1910

21. Dish, painted in *famille verte* colours with the sage Chang Kuo.
Mark, a shell. Reign of K'ang Hsi. D. 15½ in. Salting Bequest.

c. 1153–1910

22. Vase, painted in *famille verte* colours, with the Pavilion of
the Blest. Reign of K'ang Hsi. Ht. 10¼ in. Salting Bequest.

c. 1264–1910

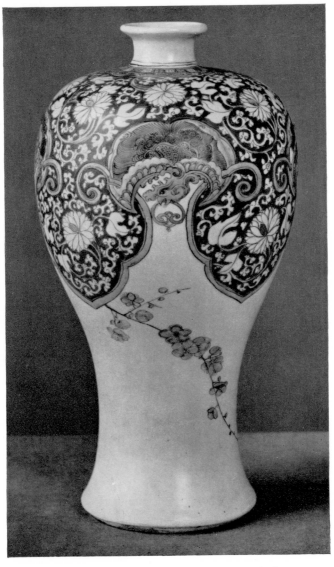

23. Vase, painted in *famille verte* colours. Reign of K'ang Hsi.
Ht. 8⅞ in. Salting Bequest.   c. 1184–1910

24. Dish, painted in *famille rose* colours. Mark and reign of Yung Chêng. D. 20 in. Couling Bequest.   c. 719–1907

25. Vase, painted with dragons, in underglaze blue: yellow ground. Reign of Yung Chêng. Ht. 26 in. Salting Bequest.

c. 995–1910

26. Plate, painted in *famille rose* colours; ruby back. Reign of Yung Chêng. D. 7⅞ in. Salting Bequest.   c. 1429–1910

27. Plate, painted in black, red and gold. Reign of Ch'ien Lung.
D. 8¾ in.   c. 33–1912

28. Vase, with landscape panels painted in *famille rose* colours; grey-green celadon ground. Mark and reign of Ch'ien Lung. Ht. 14¼ in. Salting Bequest.   c. 1466–1910